MW00928773

FUNDAMENTALS OF MICROBLADING FOR COSMETIC TATTOOISTS

EYEBROW FEATHERING ESSENTIALS

WHY YOU SHOULD READ THIS BOOK

If you are new to the world of cosmetic tattooing, or if you are keen on ongoing education, then this text will help to supplement your understanding of the microblading process.

Microblading or feather eyebrow tattooing is an increasingly popular beauty treatment. Ensuring that you are well trained in the theory and technique of this process is something that should not be compromised.

Skillful technicians are more capable, practice with more confidence, and will operate a successful business in an environment where reputation is critical.

INTRODUCTION

The eyebrow feathering or microblading tattoo technique has been practised for decades to create simulated hairstrokes for clients. Using a manual hand held tool as opposed to traditional tattooing machines, the technique requires a degree of artistic ability and understanding of skin types, coloring and facial structure.

With the rising popularity of social media, an abundance of tranformative before and after pictures of feathered eyebrows has driven demand for the treatment. Talented cosmetic tattooists have had their portfolios widely shared and made viral online. This has resulted in an influx of bookings and renewed interest in the industry.

Whilst this movement has been great for the profession, the often unregulated nature of cosmetic tattooing leaves consumers at risk of botched jobs. Poorly qualified trainers have set up two day microblading courses to capitalise on the trend. As skill levels vary largely between technicians, there is a need to maintain the reputation of the industry. This guide is by no means an attempt to wholly emcompass all that is required to operate as a cosmetic tattooist, rather, it intends to supplement existing knowledge and prevent common mistakes from happening.

Supplementary textbooks available on the market appear to focus on the field as a whole. This guide aims to cover microblading specifically in order to broach the subject in more depth. Operating as an ethical tattooist requires continuous education and a desire for ongoing development. We hope that this book supports you on this path.

TABLE OF CONTENTS

CHAPTER 1. WHAT IS MICROBLADING?

There are a wide range of terms used to describe this technique, the more general being microblading, feather eyebrow tattooing, eyebrow embroidery, to the glamourized terms of 3D brows, 6D effect etc.

Whilst the terms may vary, they all broadly refer to the same process whereby a tattooist applies colored pigment to a client's eyebrows using a fine bladed hand tool. Unlike standard eyebrow tattoos, this method is semi-permanent and can last up to three years. With the microblading technique, a more natural look is achieved as it aims to simulate hair strokes rather than a full shaded or block effect.

This method is ideal for clients who want to naturally enhance the look of their eyebrows. People suffering from alopecia, those who have over plucked, or who have sparse eyebrow hair growth can benefit greatly from microblading.

The results are natural and shaped fuller looking brows. The tattoo will initially appear darker but fade significantly during the healing process. A touch up appointment is required at a minimum of 6 weeks later to address any inconsistent healing. Following this, a touch up once a year is recommended to retain the shape and saturation of pigment.

CHAPTER 2. DIFFERENCE BETWEEN MACHINE AND MICROBLADING

Traditionally, tattoo machines have been used to create permanent solutions for those wanting defined eyebrows. Although hair strokes can be created by a 1-liner needle on a machine, this method is not as common in practice. This technique creates a larger wound than you would obtain from microblading. The hair strokes are more likely to implant using this method and tend to last longer.

However, 1-liner results are not as natural looking as you would obtain from microblading as it is difficult to create fine strokes. The hair strokes created using a hand tool will heal crisper and sharper in nature.

It is largely up to technician preference as to which tools they use. Some tattooists may change between the two options based on the client and their skin type or retention factors. For clients with larger pores and oily skin, it may be more advantageous to use the machine as implanting pigment can be difficult with a hand tool. Alternatively, you can use the microblading technique whilst managing the expectations of the client – advise that they are likely to require more than one touch up appointment for best results.

CHAPTER 3. SAFE WORKING PRACTICES

Taking a highly vigilant approach to sanitation is essential for the cosmetic tattooist. In all permanent cosmetic procedures, you will come into contact with blood or bodily fluids and their associated risks.

Without aiming to be an exhaustive list, the following outlines minimum safety standards which should be adhered to in practice:

- Working in alignment with the standards set by your local Health Department
- Undertaking study or a certification regarding blood borne pathogens
- Working from an appropriate location which prevents cross contamination, has proper waste disposal and hand washing facilities, and all areas are well sanitized
- Use of protective barriers on all tools and areas of exposure
- Appropriate outer wear such as eye protection, closed toe shoes, disposable gloves and aprons

Getting in touch with industry organizations or committees will also help you in keeping informed. Personal and client safety is not an area which can be compromised, ensure that you maintain best practice standards at all times.

CHAPTER 4. CHOOSING CLIENTS AND CONTRAINDICATIONS

When operating ethically as a cosmetic tattooist, the choice of taking on a client is as important as them choosing you to perform the treatment.

Every so often, those with contraindications or existing medical conditions may be quite insistent on an eyebrow tattoo. However, you will be putting their health at risk and damaging your brand if there is a poor outcome. The legal risks of having a problematic treatment is also something to remain vigilant of when taking on clients.

Understanding your client's history is the best way to inform both parties about their suitability for microblading. This is best done through an ad hoc discussion as well as the completion of a detailed form.

Some of the most common factors to consider are:

- Current use of Retin A or active skincare ingredients such as alpha or beta hydroxyls
- Use of blood thinning drugs or high pressure medications
- History of keloid or hypertrophic scarring
- Certain ethic groups are more prone to hyperpigmentation. This may fade over time, but it is important to flag early on with the client
- Allergies to ingredients in topical numbing creams, metals (such as Nickel), and latex in gloves

Microblading is not recommended for clients in these categories:

- Pregnant or nursing
- Botox or fillers in the brow or upper face area
- Diabetic or those with autoimmune disorders due to thinned blood and poor healing
- Taken Accutane in the past 1.5 years as the skin has not regulated
- Organ transplant as they may have compromised immune systems
- Chemotherapy in the past year
- Diseases or viral infections
- Epileptic as seizures may be induced by pain

CHAPTER 5. LIGHTING

The significance of adequate lighting in your cosmetic tattooing practice is often underrated. This is despite it being highly influential in the final treatment result.

Many work environments utilize florescent lighting. Unbeknownst to many, this form of lighting can distort your choice of pigment as well as the client's perception of chosen color. For an outcome that is most reflective of how a tattoo will appear in "real" life, ensure that your workspace has full spectrum natural lighting. This enables you to view skin undertones against pigment choice more accurately. Daylight allows you to better distinguish between differing and muted shades of color. Another advantage of this form of lighting is that is aids in minimizing eye strain over time. For those busy tattooists, this is a big pro when you are working long hours.

In terms of direct lighting, there are a number of options which are tailored for purpose. This text prefers not to mention specific brands as opinions vary greatly. However, consider the following as guidelines when selecting your equipment:

- LED full spectrum white light (recommended)
- Use of a floor lamp or headlamp
- Reduction of eye strain and glare
- Low emission of heat for client comfort
- Good balance of contrast and color fidelity
- Accessibility of purchasing replacement globes
- The inclusion of accessories such as magnifiers and clips

CHAPTER 6. TABLE SET UP

In preparation for microblading, you will need to have all elements prepared before the procedure begins. This minimizes the risk of cross contamination and also saves you time.

The typical table set up used by permanent make up artists comprises the following:

- Box of non-latex gloves
- Single use alcohol swabs
- Anesthetics
- Pigments
- Pigment cups or rings
- Microblading blade and hand tool
- Damp cotton wipes
- Cotton tips
- Micro applicators
- Eyebrow pencil
- Ruler or caliper
- Barrier tape on all non sterile surfaces
- Mirror
- Tweezers
- Mini razor
- Timer

Personal Protective Items:

- Apron
- Mouth guard
- Magnifier or protective eyewear

CHAPTER 7. MICROBLADING TOOLS

There is a widespread range of tools for microblading on the market with varying degrees of quality. The needle used by each tattooist will vary according to hair stroke pattern and individual preference.

The most important concept when picking a needle is ensuring that all blade tips are undamaged and that high quality manufacturing and sterilization techniques (such as gamma rays) were used.

Secondly, the tattooist needs to assess whether a flexible or hard type blade is more suited for the client's skin. Flexible needles are commonly used in practice as they can create more realistic hair strokes. The ability to curve each stroke is easier (due to finer needles) and this tool can be used on more skin types.

Fig 1. Examples of smaller flexible and thicker hard microblading needles

Hard type blades should be reserved for more difficult skin types such as thick or oily textures. These needles are slightly larger and create bolder strokes.

Within the range of flexible and hard blades, tattooists also need to select a needle configuration. This comes down to:

- **Needle Size** ranging from #7 to #22. Note that as the needle size rises, so too does the intensity of strokes and pigment implantation/boldness of final tattoo
- **Needle Tip** formation which can be curved, u-shaped, or straight. Tattooists should trial each type against their microblading technique to find the most comfortable match

Ensure that you use only individually packaged, sterile single-use blades. The blades will then need to be placed at an appropriate angle on a microblading pen. These pens are formed from plastic or stainless steel, with some being disposable and others able to be sterilized in an autoclave or similar apparatus.

Some factors to consider when building your toolkit include:

- Ease of assembly and clean up (if not disposable)
- Whether the tool is complementary to your microblading technique i.e. some tattooists prefer using lighter plastic pens
- Pricing of tools compared to treatment fee
- If the tool has any safety mechanisms for the technician

CHAPTER 8. ASSEMBLY AND USE OF MICROBLADING HAND TOOL

1. Prepare your sterile hand tool by screwing open and loosening the top

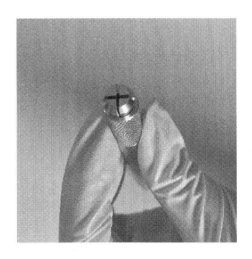

2. Carefully remove the blade from the pack, ensuring that you do not touch the needles. Pull out using the back handle of the blade

3. Secure the blade into the hand tool at a slight angle. The longest part of the blade should be positioned away from the hand tool. Ensure that it is screwed on tightly

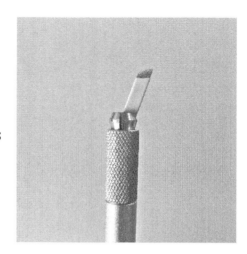

4. *INCORRECT ANGLE*

When applying your hair strokes, keep your hand tool 90° degrees upright to the client's skin and avoid leaning. You should be controlling each stroke using your wrist

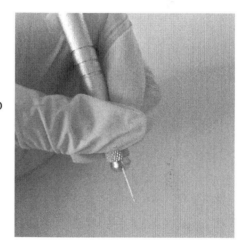

5. *CORRECT ANGLE*

You will hear a soft scratching noise and feel a moderate degree of tension against the skin. Use your opposing fingers to stretch the skin as tightly as you can. This creates more distinct strokes

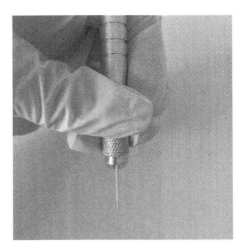

CHAPTER 9. PIGMENTS

Microblading has come a long way from traditional tattoo methods, whereby technicians would inject vegetable dyes under the skin or use body art pigments on the face. These days most pigments are formulated using carbon or iron oxide based ingredients. There are now a wide range of pigments available on the market for cosmetic tattooing, each with varying degrees of quality. Today's formulations have improved significantly from those used in previous decades. The fear of having bright blue or red eyebrows is not as concerning of late, with better testing, regulation and manufacturing of ingredients.

The choice of which pigment line to use is up to tattooist preference. Certain brands are well known for use during feathering as they tend to heal well with the blading technique. A number of high profile microblading trainers have also formulated their own pigment lines which are tailored for purpose. To assess whether a particular brand is for you, a good approach would be to review feedback and before/after shots on microblading focused Facebook groups. Some guidelines to follow when picking a brand are:

- Shelf life of pigments
- Price of pigments against the number of applications per bottle
- Whether the container design promotes sterility
- Range of shades available as well as the addition of corrective pigments
- How true to color certain pigments appear when healed. The best lines do not change in undertone when applied

- The percentage of glycerin to distilled water and alcohol in the formulation. Higher amounts of glycerin (creates a thicker, more viscous texture) in a pigment line is suited to microblading as it prevents your mixture from drying out too fast
- Quality of support materials or guidelines for use
- Accessibility of representatives from the pigment company. On occasion, you may need to ask them questions about ingredients (for clients who are allergic) or have queries about the likely outcome of color for certain skin types or nationalities

Ensure that you use only one brand and understand how to mix and manipulate pigments to form a desired color. Do not mix formulations from different lines as this may result in a muddy outcome.

Additional Tips when using Pigment

- Store bottles in a dark area and ensure that the lids are enclosed well
- Ensure that you shake the pigment bottles for at least 30 seconds to a minute before pouring out. This allows for adequate dispersion of particles
- If adding corrector shades to a base pigment, invest in a pigment mixer for best results
- When selecting a color for a client, do not gauge shade through the bottle as it can be distorted through plastic or opaque packaging. Use the color chart provided by the manufacturer and swab a test patch onto the client's forehead

Selection of Pigments for Microblading

A cosmetic tattooist must consider a number of variables when choosing a color for their client. The key factors to take into account are skin undertone (warm, neutral or cool), the existing eyebrow color (check if client has eyebrow tinting), and the client's preference for color.

The resultant choice for pigment color will need to complement the above criteria. This requires an understanding of how the pigment interacts with certain skin types, i.e. those with Fitzpatrick skin types II to VI may heal darker than the pigment applied. The technician will need to consider this pre-treatment and adjust their selection accordingly.

It is highly recommended that permanent cosmetic artists undertake fundamental color theory and skin undertone training. This topic is generally not addressed adequately in basic PMU training, despite it being core to a successful outcome for your client.

CHAPTER 10. PRACTICING HAIR STROKES

The microblading technique requires tattooists to extend their artistic abilities past that of simply shaping eyebrows. Replicating hair strokes to achieve a natural result demands practice and an understanding of hair growth patterns.

Each feathering course will recommend differing methods of applying strokes. Some base their patterns on cultural background (Asian style, European style etc.), whilst others attest that you should master and use the same style for all clients. The type of hair stroke each technician uses largely comes down to individual preference and their success in implanting pigment using their method. As such, this text does not provide direction as to how each person should microblade, rather, we recommend some methods of practicing technique.

Latex Practice Mats - Readily purchased from tattoo suppliers, these blank mats aim to replicate the texture of human skin. On the blank mat, use an eyebrow pencil to draw an outline of a set of symmetrical brows. Proceed to microblade the shape with your preferred needle. Wet wipes can be used to remove excess pigment and view your strokes

Pig Skin - Similar in concept to the latex mats, pig skin is also a realistic practicing option. Purchase this from your butcher and use a razor to shave off any hair. Note that pig skin will dry out within a few hours and is a single use item (unless you purchase in bulk and freeze). Practice microblading in the same way as you would with a latex mat

Black Carbon Paper - Available at most stationary or office suppliers, this paper is traditionally used for receipts and invoice books. The advantage of carbon paper is that it clearly reflects the hair stroke pattern; any poorly placed strokes will stand out. This method will also allow technicians to gauge the depth of their hair strokes and adjust accordingly. To use, proceed to microblade the paper lightly without the use of pigments

Eyebrow Templates or Drawing - Although this method does not compare to human skin, do not underestimate the value of freehand drawing of eyebrow patterns. Technicians should constantly be practicing whilst on the go, with the eyebrow template (printed brow outlines) or paper turned in the direction in which the client faces during their treatment

Of course the best type of practice comes from taking on actual clients. The confidence achieved from a great result allows you to tweak your technique and continuously improve.

CHAPTER 11. SKIN ANATOMY

The skin is the largest organ of the body and serves a variety of functions. As the canvas for eyebrow tattooing, understanding the skin and the function of each layer is essential for the permanent cosmetic technician.

The skin strata are divided into 3 layers. In descending order, they are:

Epidermis
The outermost layer of dead skin cells which are visible to the naked eye. It varies in thickness throughout the body and functions as a protective barrier that interfaces with the external environment and its pathogens.

Dermis
The middle layer of the skin which contains many specialized cells and structures. Hair follicles, sebaceous oil glands, sweat glands, and nerve cells are present here. The dermis is connected to the epidermis though a tight structure of collagen, elastic fibers and reticular fibers.

Hypodermis
The deepest layer of the skin. It stores fat (adipose) tissue which functions as a shock absorber, protecting the internal organs from injury and also providing insulation.

Common microblading mistakes occur when tattooists implant only in the epidermal layer, causing clients to return with virtually no retention. Understanding the depth at which to place strokes requires practice and ongoing feedback from seeing healed results.

Experienced technicians have a grasp of the *sweet spot* whereby feathering doesn't pull too deep into the hypodermis (causing bleeding and a blurred blue-grey healed result) or too lightly, where they have only skimmed the surface of the skin.

For microblading, the optimal area of pigment implantation is beneath the epidermal basal cell layer (in the upper reticular layer of the dermis). This ensures that the tattoo will not disappear during the cellular renewal process.

CHAPTER 12. TATTOOING OVER SCARS

On occasion, permanent makeup technicians will encounter a client with some form of scarring. This scenario is particularly common in microblading as individuals are looking for solutions to conceal a gap or wound caused by the scar. There is no precise yes or no to the practice of feathering over this form of skin tissue, rather, it requires an educated assessment of the result.

Some technicians have successfully implanted hair strokes over scarring, whilst others report that the healed results are poor. A key difficulty with taking on clients with scar tissue is that the inner composition of damaged skin is not visible to the naked eye. It can be a combination of guesswork and experience as to whether it is worth a try. Notwithstanding this, there are some guidelines which can help technicians in their assessment.

What are Scars?

Scars are areas of fibrous tissue that take the place of normal skin after injury to the dermis. They are formed from the same type of protein as unharmed skin but are composed of different fibrous patterns. The functional quality of scar tissue is lower with it being unable to regenerate hair follicles or sweat glands. The distorted arrangement of collagen also causes scars to be less resistant to ultra violet radiation; even if pigment successfully implants in the scar tissue, the longevity of the tattoo is poorer than that of normal tattooed skin after sun exposure.

To Microblade or not?

When presented with a case of scarring, it is always beneficial to manage the expectations of your client upfront. Communicate to them why there is a risk of poor pigment retention when tattooing over scar tissue. In the event of nerve damage where the scar is, the client may also be prone to experiencing more discomfort from a tattoo. If you are particularly concerned, then request that the client produce a medical clearance from their dermatologist or practitioner.

The following factors can aid in your assessment of whether to proceed with the microblading:

- Scar should be at least one year old and stable in appearance
- The scar texture should be unraised, smooth and relatively flat. Avoid keloid scarring
- If the color of the scar is red or pink, it may still be healing and best left untouched
- If the scar has an obvious border or darkened edge, then this may indicate post-inflammatory hyper pigmentation. Tattooing over the scar can actually worsen the appearance of the darkness

Chapter 13. Microblading Technique & Steps

1. Set up your workspace in a sanitary manner. Affix barrier film on all surfaces that are likely to be touched during the procedure

2. Once the client arrives, check that their skin is free from cuts, abrasions and any infection

3. Wipe client eyebrows clean with an alcohol swab and take a before photograph. Apply a topical anesthetic for the prescribed timeframe. Cover the area with cling film to enhance absorption. The client should have a slight halo around their eyebrows once numbed

4. Whilst waiting for the numbing cream to absorb, consult with the client about their desired outcome. Talk them through the process and offer to answer any questions

5. Bring the client into the treatment room and wipe away the excess numbing cream. Use a clean or sharpened pencil to design the eyebrow shape. Using a ruler or caliper, check that each side is symmetrical and even in length. Ensure that the client is happy with the shape and thickness

6. Based on their skin tone, undertone, and existing hair and eyebrow color, select an appropriate pigment. Swab this onto the client's forehead and check for approval. Although the final healed color will look different once merged into the skin, this is the closest method of assessing fit

7. Put on necessary protective gear including a face mask, gloves and apron. You can wear eye googles or magnifiers once you commence with tattooing

8. Mix your pigment and add correctors if required. Prepare your feathering hand tool. Present the packaged blade to the client and assure them that all tools are sterile and disposable

9. Commence with your feather strokes. It is very important to secure your drawn eyebrow template in the first pass. Maintain a good stretch and follow your drawing. Do not use too much pigment or you will mask your stroke pattern. There should be minimal bleeding if any. Adjust your pressure if you do encounter blood

10. Once you have finished the first pass, saturate the brow with pigment and rub it in to soak with a micro applicator. The client may experience mild stinging as the pigment penetrates into their skin

11. Move onto the opposite eyebrow and repeat the steps

12. Once you have finished the second brow, the first brow should have had adequate time to absorb the pigment - 5 to 10 minutes. Wipe away the color and apply numbing agent which is formulated for broken skin. Commence your second microblading pass after the anesthetic absorbs (timeframe according to product instructions). Soak pigment into the eyebrow

13. Repeat the wipe, numb, tattooing and pigment soaking process with the second eyebrow. Ensure that you apply

the anesthetic sparingly or as needed. Excessive use of numbing agents will cause dilution of pigment and impact the healed outcome

14. Sit your client up to check for symmetry and mark if additional hair strokes or shape adjustments are required

15. Ensure that your pigment mixture is well combined as the liquid suspension can separate or dry out over time. Keep mixing the pot or ring

16. Reapply numbing agent if client is uncomfortable. Microblade final adjustments and allow pigment to soak for 10 minutes. Talk client through the aftercare process and typical healing pattern whilst waiting

17. Remove all pigment. Sit client up and take after photos

18. Apply aftercare product and provide client with print out of aftercare steps

19. Book client in for touch up session and you are finished!

CHAPTER 14. AFTERCARE

There are a range of aftercare options and approaches, with none being clearly preferred in the industry. This is because of the diversity of skin types and products available in different areas. In any case, it is important to provide an aftercare instruction sheet to clients and talk them through the steps.

Permanent make up artists typically take one of the following approaches to aftercare:

Dry Healing: Applying a transparent barrier cream such as Cavilon over the tattoo immediately after the treatment. The client is advised not to wet the area for 3 to 4 days and avoid exposure to hot steam. Following this time, the client is given an emollient such as grape seed or rosehip oil to apply onto their eyebrows for the next 7 days (in a thin layer both in the morning and night). This assists in the promotion of healing and helps to seal in the pigment

Moist Healing: Clients are advised to apply either an antibiotic cream, Bepanthen or Vaseline to their eyebrows using a clean cotton tip applicator. This should be done at least 3 times a day to ensure that the area does not dry out. Clients should discontinue with application once their tattoo begins to exfoliate

CHAPTER 15. REMOVAL AND CORRECTIONS

As a permanent makeup artist, you will often encounter clients with faded and discolored tattoos. These individuals may be looking for a coverage solution or some advice on removal. To assess whether you can microblade over the existing tattoo, some factors to consider are:

The density of old pigment and if it is too dark or discolored (blue and red hues are quite common) to tattoo over. Also note that a significant degree of fading will occur upon healing and thus the old tattoo can become visible again. Ensure that you communicate this risk to the client

How long ago the procedure was undertaken. If it is a recent case where the client is not happy with the result, then you may advise for them to try an at home solution. Using retinol or hydroxyl acids, or scrubbing with manual exfoliants can help to promote fading. If the tattoo is a few years old, then you can be fairly confident that any residual pigment is stable and will not change significantly within the next few months. You can make a removal assessment based on what you observe

In the event that an existing tattoo is too dense to cover, a client has a number of options:

Dermabrasion: Somewhat dated method which manually removes the skin layers using a sanding device. The higher risk of scarring and skin trauma associated with dermabrasion led the way for less evasive measures like laser

Laser Removal: A medical procedure undertaken by trained professionals. This method has a high degree of effectiveness if performed right using quality lasers. Note that multiple sessions may be required to achieve a desired outcome. For those clients who have been tattooed with a titanium dioxide based pigment (usually a skin tone color with a whitened appearance), laser is not an option as the tattoo will turn black and oxidize during the treatment

Saline and Salt Removal: Only to be performed by trained permanent cosmetic artists. This form of removal can be used for both lightening of old tattoos or corrections for current clients (for example if you misplace a hair stroke). It involves the use of a traditional digital or rotary tattoo machine and a removal solution. This solution is composed of a sterile saline and salt mixture. It can either be formulated by the tattooist or purchased in a premixed format. As with laser removal, this method is likely to require more than one session for effective results. Clients will appear red and scabbed following this form of treatment. A minimum time frame of 8 weeks between treatments is recommended to allow for healing

Color Correction: Adding a new pigment which will counteract the color of the existing tattoo. Tattooists must be well trained in color theory to undertake this treatment. It is often not recommended as there is no certainty in knowing what pigment components were used in the original tattoo – these may react poorly with any new attempts at coverage

If you will be performing removals in any capacity, ensure that this is stipulated in your insurance cover. Many policies fail to factor in this treatment under the framework of cosmetic tattooing.

Also be wary of the expectations of your client. Removals are a stressful and long process which can take a toll on both parties. Ensure that there is clear communication about the number of treatments required as well as likely results. When in doubt, it is better to protect yourself and refer on to more specialized parties.

CHAPTER 16. MAINTENANCE OF EYEBROW TATTOO

There are a number of factors which can influence the final healed outcome of a microbladed eyebrow. These can be environmental, procedural and/or individual factors. Some of the key influencing factors are listed below:

Sun Exposure - Clients who live active lifestyles and are regularly in the sun may experience a faster fading of color. Pigment particles are broken down by exposure to ultra violet rays. Daily use of sunscreen is essential in prevention of premature tattoo fading or color change

Skin Type - Microblading is highly influenced by skin type. Those with very oily skin and large pores are unlikely to get a satisfactory result as excess sebum may push out pigment. Tattooists should adjust the blade type accordingly for clients based on their skin

Client Age - Older clients often have tougher skin and require larger needle configurations to implant strokes. They may also take longer to heal

Medical Background - The overall health profile of the client can affect the tattoo outcome. Certain medications can thin out blood, whilst underlying medical conditions may affect the person's immune system. Conversely, clients with exceptional immune systems may find this to be counterproductive; their body is adept at removal of foreign substances and may break down pigment particles quicker

Tattoo Application - The blade chosen and pressure used by the technician can greatly influence retention. They may deposit minimal pigment at the dermal level, as such, impacting the length of time that the tattoo will last

Chapter 17. Client Healing

Following a microblading procedure, there is an expected sequence of healing behaviors within the skin. You should familiarize yourself with this process to ensure that you can comprehensively brief your clients. Emphasize upfront to clients that microbladed eyebrows are temperamental in healing; it will take up to 6 weeks until a final result can be affirmed. Although there are often differences between skin types and nationality of clients, the general trend of healing is as follows:

Day 1

The client may experience some swelling in the area which typically resolves soon after the treatment. There may be residual plasma or blood clotting over the tattoo. This is the result of the body's healing process when a wound is inflicted. Eyebrows will appear up to 50% darker and more intense in color. This is due to pigment implanting in the upper layer of the epidermis which will eventually flake off.

Days 2-3

The eyebrows will begin to scab and hair strokes feel somewhat raised when touched. Clients will experience itching as the skin starts to heal itself. It is critical that the client does not pick or scratch the eyebrows as this will impact pigment retention (i.e. hair strokes may heal in patches).

Days 4-7

Scabbing and eventual flaking of the eyebrows will occur until they no longer feel raised. The itching sensation should be minimized once the skin has fully exfoliated. Clients may be concerned that there is little color retention at this point due to masking by the epidermal layer of the skin.

Days 8-40

The pigment implanted in the upper dermis will solidify and a touch up of the eyebrows can be undertaken at the 6-week point. Assess where additional hair strokes or pigment adjustments are required.

Chapter 18. Common Microblading Mistakes To Avoid

There are a number of common mistakes that permanent makeup artists make when microblading. Although many will encounter these issues in practice, this book aims to prevent you from learning the hard way. Ensure you remain conscious of the following when working on clients:

- Do not design an eyebrow shape whilst tattooing, even if you are just filling in sparseness. The canvas is likely to change as the skin swells or becomes irritated during the procedure. This is poor practice which increases the risk of asymmetries and client complaints. Always pre-mark out your outline

- Having a poor stretching technique will distort the symmetry and implantation of your pigment. Ensure that you master your three finger stretch as this both minimizes discomfort for the client, and allows you to microblade into the correct depth of the skin

- Continue mixing your pigment during the treatment so that all components are well distributed. This small step can make the difference between a well healed result and one that is patchy

- Avoid excessive application of anesthetics. This will dilute the pigment and can cause patchiness in healed results. Assess the required amount of numbing agent on a case by case basis; clients with a high pain tolerance may even bypass this step

- If you are having issues with the hair strokes not appearing on the skin, it may be due to a blunt or damaged needle tip. This exacerbates the pain experienced by clients and also affects the implantation of strokes. Wipe your blade and if it collects some of the tissue then change immediately. Alternatively, use a magnifier or eye loop to examine your blade

- Not waiting long enough for touch ups in older clientele. Due to immune factors and more porous skin, it may take slightly longer (8 or more weeks) to see a final result in this age group. Women from 50 years and onwards often scab up later in the healing process. Assess this on a client by client basis

- Maintain a log of the dates in which your consumables expire. Many pigments and anesthetics must be used within a particular timeframe after opening. Using dated materials can cause irregularities in color and application

- Allowing clients to bring friends or partners into the treatment room. You will find that this consumes more time as they are checking with their peer for validation, as well as chatting and moving their face whilst you are trying to draw or microblade. You do not need an additional person present to scrutinize your work. Reserve the treatment room to just you and your client for "hygiene reasons" (which is also a legitimate cause!)

- Don't skip on personal hygiene. Awkward but true, as a cosmetic tattooist you will work quite intimately with clients. Bad body odor can make a client's experience horrible. Use deodorant and shower regularly, this is a non negotiable

Conclusion

Over the course of your career as a permanent make up technician, you will inevitably learn some hard lessons through practice. Many of us encounter complaints, reputational damage (particularly in this social media obsessed world), and demotivating days where nothing goes right. Staying in this field requires tattooists to develop a strong degree of resilience.

Having a support network of colleagues in the same field is often helpful to compare experiences. Those who prevail and stay on in this business often find their profession highly rewarding, both from a client satisfaction and monetary perspective. All the best on your microblading endeavors and be grateful that you are part of an ever expanding industry!

ONE LAST THING...

If you enjoyed this book or found it useful I'd be very grateful if you'd post a short review on Amazon. Your support really does make a difference and I read all the reviews personally so I can get your feedback and make this book even better.

Thanks again for your support

Made in the USA
San Bernardino, CA
05 October 2016